TRANSPORTATION
TRANSPORTATION

Troll Associates

TRANSPORTATION
TRANSPORTATION

by Keith Brandt

Illustrated by Rex Schneider

Troll Associates

Library of Congress Cataloging in Publication Data

Brandt, Keith, (date)
    Transportation.

    Summary: Describes the vehicles people have used to
carry themselves and their things from place to place
throughout history, from the Stone Age sledge through
modern aircraft and submarines.
        1. Transportation—History—Juvenile literature.
[1. Transportation—History.   2. Vehicles—History]
I. Schneider, Rex, ill.   II. Title.
HE152.B67   1984   380.5   84-2584
ISBN 0-8167-0172-5 (lib. bdg.)
ISBN 0-8167-0173-3 (pbk.)

When cold weather comes and birds want to go south, they must fly there. Their wings provide them with transportation through the air. When the grass is gone in one feeding area, deer must walk to another grassy place. Their feet provide them with transportation across the land.

And when a salmon wants to go upstream and lay its eggs, it must swim there. Its tail and fins provide it with transportation through the water. But when human beings want to get from one place to another, they can choose from many forms of transportation.

On land, a human being can walk, ride a bike, drive a car, catch a bus, grab a cab, take a train. To travel through the air, a person can hop on a plane, go up in a helicopter, use a hang-glider, rise in a hot-air balloon! And to get across the water, people can float or swim, ride on a raft or sail in a boat, board a big steamship, or travel below the surface in a submarine.

Dozens of different vehicles are used for transportation. There are ambulances, police cars, and fire engines. There are

trains that travel across a whole country and planes that fly faster than the speed of sound.

People can take a short trip over water on a ferry, or cruise around the world on a ship that is like a floating hotel. Some people have even traveled to the moon and back in a spacecraft.

Transportation takes us where we want to go. It carries people from place to place. But transportation is not limited to carrying people.

Transportation carries *things*. Trains, trucks, ships, and planes carry farm products and candy bars, newspapers and crude oil, toys and games, clothing and furniture, TV sets and cassette players, sporting goods and library books. Transportation brings us the things we eat, drink, wear, use, sleep on, and play with. It brings us just about everything we need.

Transportation has changed greatly over the years. For many thousands of years our early ancestors had no sort of transportation at all. They traveled only as far as they could walk. When they wanted to take something with them, they dragged it or carried it.

Then, about 8,000 years ago, people began transporting things on a sledge. A sledge is a kind of sled that can be pulled over the ground. The first sledges were probably hollowed-out tree trunks that Stone Age hunters used to bring their food back home. And in time, when these early humans began keeping horses and oxen, they used these animals to pull heavily loaded sledges.

But sledges, even when they had smooth runners on the bottom, weren't very good. They bumped and dragged along the ground. They turned over easily and were hard to move over rough surfaces or up and down hills.

The problem was partly solved by rolling a sledge over logs. But this meant someone had to pick up the logs that the sledge had already rolled over, and put them ahead of the sledge again. Doing that over and over was a lot of work!

Then the wheel was invented. The first wheels may have been thin slices of a log, or they may have been circles cut out of wooden planks or boards. The wheel was an important invention. It made life so much easier that the idea spread far and wide in a very short time.

With wheeled vehicles, people could move things long distances much more easily. They could load large quantities of goods into wheeled carts or wagons that were pulled by animals. This made trade possible. Soon roads began to crisscross the countrysides.

The Romans built the first system of paved roads. Their stone-surfaced roads joined together the most distant parts of the Roman Empire. The ancient Romans sped along in horse-drawn chariots. But after the fall of the Roman Empire, there was little long-distance land transportation for hundreds of years.

Throughout the Middle Ages, there were few good roads, and it was simply too dangerous for most people to travel very far. Thieves and robbers lay in wait for those who dared to travel overland.

Of course, people didn't travel only by land. Our early ancestors may have started using water transportation by accident.

Maybe someone fell into a river, grabbed onto a floating log, and held on until reaching safety.

Soon, people began tying logs together to make rafts and steering them with poles or paddles. Next, they may have hollowed out logs and, later, learned how to make canoes. Then larger boats were built, and goods were shipped long distances over water.

Transportation by water was easier and faster than land transportation. Because of this, great cities grew along the coasts and along inland waterways.

Then, in the nineteenth century, a steam engine was developed that brought about great changes in all forms of transportation. Steamships did not have to wait for the wind like sailing ships did. Instead, they simply fired up their engines and steamed across the water.

On land, steam locomotives pulled railroad trains across the country in a few days. It had taken many weeks for the same trip to be made in a covered wagon pulled by animals.

The gasoline engine, or internal-combustion engine, was another important development in the history of transportation. Less than one hundred years have passed since Henry Ford first began making the inexpensive Model T automobile. Yet today, cars and trucks are everywhere.

At first, these "horseless carriages" were driven along dirt or gravel roads. But as the use of motor vehicles grew, so did the need

for better driving conditions. Soon gravel and dirt roads were paved. Roads were widened and divided into lanes.

As speeds increased, traffic rules were established and enforced by signs, lights, and police. Networks of superhighways were built to move traffic quickly and efficiently. Bridges and tunnels were built to carry traffic over and under water and through mountains.

Roads, bridges, and tunnels always need repair, so tolls are charged for each vehicle, and road taxes are collected. For the sake of safety, vehicles that use public roads must be registered, drivers must pass a test to get a license, and many places require regular auto inspections. The automobile has changed our laws, the landscape, and the way we live.

Equally important was the invention of the airplane. Since the Wright brothers' first successful flight in 1903, the airplane has shortened travel time across continents or oceans from days to hours.

Today there are thousands of flights in and out of huge international airports and small local airports. To make sure that all this air traffic is handled smoothly and safely, governments all over the world cooperate on rules and regulations. Takeoffs and landings are scheduled with care, weather information is shared, and there is constant radio communication to avoid dangers.

The history of transportation is also the history of fuels. When animals were used to pull vehicles, their fuel was their daily food and water. The steam engine burned wood or coal, and that was a big advance. Then came the gasoline engine, which could do more work on less fuel.

But gasoline comes from oil, which someday will be used up. So there is a growing need for new fuels for transportation. What will they be? Solar energy? Electricity? Nuclear energy? No one knows for sure. For that matter, no one knows what the vehicles of the future will be.

It takes great imagination to think up and develop any new means of transportation. Hundreds of years ago, the Italian genius Leonardo da Vinci drew plans for a submarine and a helicopter.

But it wasn't until a little more than a century ago that practical submarines were built and successful cigar-shaped airships called blimps arrived—soon to be overshadowed by the airplane. Yet even this great invention had its failures. There was the steam aircraft that never got off the ground. And there were a number of unworkable flying machines powered by humans flapping their arms.

But imagination has led to many successes, too. Today there are hovercraft that go on land and water, using a cushion of air. There are hydrofoils that skim over water on underwater wings called struts. There are monorails, or trains that ride on one rail at remarkable speeds. And there are supersonic jet planes and rockets and the spacecraft that travel from Earth to outer space.

What's next? Only the future will answer that question.